# THE MASTERS

by Brian Howell

Printed in the United States of America,
North Mankato, Minnesota
102012
012013

 THIS BOOK CONTAINS AT LEAST 10% RECYCLED MATERIALS.

Editor: Chrös McDougall
Series Designer: Craig Hinton

**Photo Credits:** Phil Sandlin/AP Images, Cover, 46; Dave Martin/AP Images, Title, 10, 59 (bottom, left); Amy Sancetta/AP Images, 5, 51; AP Images, 7, 16, 19, 24, 26, 33, 41, 43, 49, 58 (top, left and bottom), 59 (top); Bettmann/Corbis/AP Images, 13, 37, 38, 58 (top, right), 60 (bottom); Horace Cort/AP Images, 21, 29, 31; Chris O'Meara/AP Images, 54; David J. Phillip/AP Images, 57, 59, (bottom, right); Bill Waugh/AP Images, 60 (top, left); David Cannon/Getty Images, 60 (top, right)

**Cataloging-in-Publication Data**
Howell, Brian.
The Masters / Brian Howell.
   p. cm. -- (Sports' great championships)
Includes bibliographical references and index.
ISBN 978-1-61783-670-1
1. Golf--Georgia--Juvenile literature.  2. Masters Golf Tournament--Juvenile literature.  3. Augusta National Golf Club--Juvenile literature.  I. Title.
796.352/66--dc22

2012946243

# TABLE OF CONTENTS

# Tiger Roars to Victory

S unday afternoon at the Masters has produced some of the most dramatic moments in the history of golf. In 1997, however, Eldrick "Tiger" Woods managed to take away all the drama by Saturday night.

Just 21 years old at the time, Woods took a monster nine-stroke lead after the third round. The fourth round, on Sunday afternoon, was simply a celebration of one of the great performances ever. Playing in his first major tournament as a professional, Woods won by a whopping 12 strokes over second-place Tom Kite. The annual tournament at Augusta

Tiger Woods, just 21 and competing in his first major as a professional, tees off on the first hole at Augusta National Golf Club in the 1997 Masters.

National Golf Club in Georgia had never seen such a performance—and might not ever see such dominance again.

Through 2012, that was still the largest margin of victory in Masters history. Woods finished the tournament at 18-under par. That was another record. The previous best was 17-under par by Jack Nicklaus in 1965 and tied by Raymond Floyd in 1976.

"To shoot 18-under par on this golf course, as difficult as it played all week, is an incredible feat," Kite said.

## Breaking Barriers

Everything about Woods's performance and victory from April 10 to 13, 1997, was incredible.

THE MASTERS

Augusta National Golf Club had historically been a club for white men. In fact, Masters founder Clifford Roberts once said, "As long as I'm alive, golfers will be white, and caddies will be black."

It was not until 1975 that Lee Elder became the first black golfer to play in the Masters. Augusta National did not invite its first black member until 1990. Yet seven years later Woods, who is part African-American and part Asian, was dominating the course like no one before him.

"I think that's why this victory is even more special," Woods said. "Lee Elder came here today and that meant a lot to me. He was the first.

## Golf's Majors

The Masters is one of four major tournaments played each year in men's professional golf. It is the only major played at the same course each year. The Masters is also the first major each year. It is held annually in April. The other majors are the US Open, the British Open, and the Professional Golfers' Association (PGA) Championship. Through 2012, Jack Nicklaus had won more majors (18) than any player.

He was the one I looked up to, Charlie [Sifford], all of them. Because of them, I was able to play here. I was able to live my dream because of those guys."

The performance officially began Woods's climb to golf superstardom. However, those in the golf community were already well aware of the 21-year-old.

Woods was a child prodigy who appeared on television playing golf at age two. He was a six-time winner of the Junior World Championships. He won the US Junior Amateur at 15 years old. That made him the youngest person to win that title. He later won that title two more times. Woods also became the youngest winner of the US Amateur at age 18 in 1994. He won that event three times.

The 1997 Masters was just the fifteenth professional event of Woods's career. He already had three wins at that time. But it was at Augusta National in April of 1997 that Woods really put himself on the map.

## A True Master

The four-round tournament did not start off so well in 1997. Woods shot a 4-over-par 40 on his first nine holes of the tournament. No winner of the Masters had ever done worse to start out.

"I was just hoping to make the cut," Woods said.

Woods indeed made the cut. He finished that day with a 2-under 70. Then he followed that with a 6-under 66 in round two and a 7-under 65 in round three. Veteran Colin Montgomerie played with Woods during the third round. Montgomerie admitted defeat before the fourth round.

"There is no chance," he said. "We're all human beings here. There's no chance humanly possible."

During Sunday's final round, Woods fired a 3-under 69 to put the finishing touch on a historic weekend of golf. The crowd was silent when Woods looked over a four-foot par putt on the 18th green. When the ball dropped into the cup, Woods pumped his fist and the crowd roared. He became the youngest—and most dominant—champion in the tournament's history.

Defending Masters champion Nick Faldo places the ceremonial green jacket on new Masters champion Tiger Woods in 1997.

How good was Woods during the week? He averaged 323 yards with his driver. That was 25 yards farther than anyone else. He also avoided the dreaded three-putt on all 72 holes. Woods was already being compared to Michael Jordan. Jordan was widely regarded as the best and most dominant and famous basketball player in the world.

"The bigger the event, the higher he'll raise the bar," fellow player Paul Azinger said of Woods. "He's Michael Jordan in long pants."

When it was over, Woods walked off the 18th green. He gave his father, Earl, a big hug. It was Earl who introduced his son to golf and

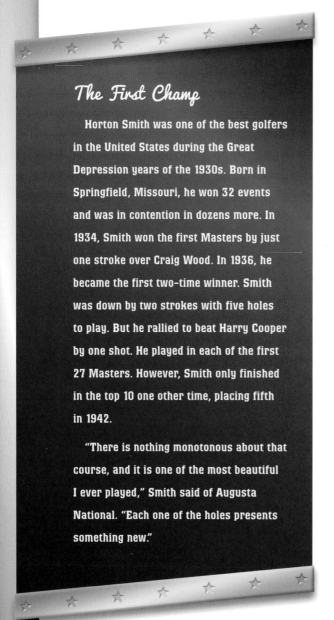

## The First Champ

Horton Smith was one of the best golfers in the United States during the Great Depression years of the 1930s. Born in Springfield, Missouri, he won 32 events and was in contention in dozens more. In 1934, Smith won the first Masters by just one stroke over Craig Wood. In 1936, he became the first two-time winner. Smith was down by two strokes with five holes to play. But he rallied to beat Harry Cooper by one shot. He played in each of the first 27 Masters. However, Smith only finished in the top 10 one other time, placing fifth in 1942.

"There is nothing monotonous about that course, and it is one of the most beautiful I ever played," Smith said of Augusta National. "Each one of the holes presents something new."

Bobby Jones was one of golf's biggest stars during the 1920s and into the 1930s. He won each of the four biggest tournaments in golf in 1930. That year, he won the US Open, the US Amateur, the British Open, and the British Amateur. Jones won the US Amateur championship five times, the US Open four times, and the British Open three times during his career.

Golf was never Jones's main priority, though. That's why he never became a professional. He was a lawyer, but played golf as an amateur. In 1930, he stunned golf fans by retiring from the game at the age of 28.

As good as Jones was as a player, his biggest contribution to golf came after his retirement. Jones was born in Atlanta, Georgia. He also got a degree from the Georgia Institute of Technology. And he worked as a lawyer in Georgia.

In 1931, Jones and Clifford Roberts purchased the Fruitland Nurseries in Augusta, Georgia. The land was filled with a lot of different types of plants and trees. However, Fruitland Nurseries had been out of business for several years. Jones saw different potential in the land.

"Perfect! And to think this ground has been lying here all these years waiting for someone to come along and lay a golf course on it," Jones said on his first visit to the land.

## Building Augusta

Right away, Jones selected Dr. Alister Mackenzie to design a golf course on the land. Mackenzie had designed several golf courses around

After three years of work, Augusta National finally opened in December 1932. The first official rounds took place in 1933.

the world. Now he set his sights on making Augusta National one of the country's finest courses. Part of Mackenzie's plan was to include many of the plants that were a part of Fruitland Nurseries. Most of those plants are still common at the golf course. In fact, each hole is named for a plant featured on that hole. One of the most popular plants is the azalea.

Jones, Roberts, and Mackenzie put a lot of effort into their plan. Augusta National Golf Club opened in December of 1932. The first official rounds at the club were played during a cold, rainy day in January of 1933.

## Shot Heard 'Round the World

The 1935 Masters provided one of the great memories in golf. Future Hall of Famer Gene Sarazen trailed with four holes to play. Then he delivered an amazing shot, holing a double eagle 2 on the par-5 15th hole. Sarazen hit a 4 wood from 235 yards out on his famous shot. That forced a tie with Craig Wood. Sarazen then won a 36-hole playoff by five shots. It was Sarazen's only Masters win. "That double eagle wouldn't have meant a thing if I hadn't won the playoff the next day," he said.

"Our overall aim at the Augusta National has been to provide a golf course of considerable natural beauty, enjoyable for the average golfer and at the same time testing for the expert player striving to better par," Jones said when the club opened.

## The Masters Begins

The first Masters tournament was held from March 22 to 25 in 1934. At the time, it was called the Augusta National Invitation Tournament. There were 72 players. The only way to get in the tournament was an invitation from Jones.

Although he did not want to, Jones was convinced by others to return to competition for the tournament. And he played quite well. Jones finished thirteenth. Horton Smith won and took home a prize of $1,500.

The tournament was also significant because it was the first time a golf tournament was broadcast to the nation on the radio.

Within five years, the Augusta National Invitation Tournament was a hit. It drew many of golf's great players and was well run. In 1939, the tournament officially became known as "the Masters." That had been an unofficial name for years, but Jones did not like it.

In the years that followed, the Masters continued to draw golf's great players. It also continued to produce great moments. Ralph Guldahl was one of the early stars at the Masters. He had won the US Open in 1937 and 1938. He was also Masters runner-up in both 1937 and 1938. At the 1939 Masters, Guldahl played a brilliant back nine in the final round. He beat Sam Snead by one stroke for his first and only Masters win.

In 1940, Jimmy Demaret won by four strokes. That was the largest margin of victory during the first 11 Masters events. The next year, Craig

Wood was the first player to lead wire to wire. That meant he had the lead after each of the four rounds. Wood had been runner-up in 1934 and 1935.

The 1942 Masters pitted two of golf's legends—Byron Nelson and Ben Hogan—against each other. Both finished the four-round event at 8-under par. So they squared off in an 18-hole playoff. Nelson shot a 69 to win the playoff by one stroke. That gave Nelson his second Masters win.

That would be the last Masters for several years. Because of World War II, the event was not held from 1943 to 1945. Although it was just nine years old before the break for war, the Masters had already established itself as one of the greatest events in sports.

# Post-War

Shortly after the 1942 Masters, Augusta National shut down. Bobby Jones and Clifford Roberts agreed that it was best to close the course during World War II. The United States had entered the war in Europe and Asia in 1941.

Jones became a captain in the US Army Air Corps. Other well-known golfers served in the military during the war, as well. Among them were Ben Hogan, Jimmy Demaret, and Sam Snead.

Jimmy Demaret pulls a rabbit out of the hole at Augusta National while a caddie looks on. Demaret won the tournament in 1940, 1947, and 1950.

Augusta National itself was used in a much different way during those years. In support of the war, approximately 200 cows and 1,400 turkeys were raised on the Augusta National grounds. The club made money by selling the meat of the turkeys to local residents. The cows kept the grass cut low but, unfortunately, they also ate a lot of the plants.

Augusta National also housed German prisoners of war (POWs). Before the club reopened, the POWs were used to fix the course that the cows damaged. The course finally reopened late in 1945. The Masters returned in the spring of 1946.

## Golfing Again

The Masters returned with another great finish. Like he did in 1942, Ben Hogan played well. But he again lost in a down-to-the-wire battle.

Herman Keiser took a five-shot lead into the final round. However, he lost it when he three-putted the final hole. That left him in a tie with Hogan, who was still on the course. When Hogan got to the 18th green, he also three-putted—missing a two-footer that would have forced a playoff. Hogan lost by one stroke. Keiser came out ahead for his only Masters win.

That was one of several great finishes during the late 1940s and 1950s. Snead, Jack Burke Jr., Arnold Palmer, and Art Wall Jr. all had one-shot victories in the 1950s. Three other Masters tournaments were decided by just two shots during that time.

Along with great finishes, the Masters showcased some of golf's great players during those years.

## Hogan v. Snead

From 1949 to 1954, Sam Snead won the Masters three times and Ben Hogan won it twice. In 1954, they squared off for the win. Both finished at 1-over par to tie for the lead at the end of four rounds. That set up an 18-hole playoff, which Snead won by one stroke. It was Snead's third Masters win. For Hogan, it was the second time he lost in a playoff (also in 1942). Through 2012, Hogan was the only player to lose a playoff twice at the Masters.

Hogan was one of them. Among his nine career major wins in his Hall of Fame career were the 1951 and 1953 Masters. Hogan's win in 1953 was the greatest performance of the first 30 years at Augusta. He finished 14-under par, breaking the tournament record by five shots. After an opening round 70, Hogan had three straight rounds in the 60s. He was the first champion in Masters history to post three sub-70 rounds.

Hogan was one of the most consistent players in Masters history. The second time he played the Masters, in 1939, he was ninth. From 1939 to 1956, he played in the Masters 14 times and never finished outside of

**THE MASTERS**

the top 10. In addition to his two wins, Hogan wound up as Masters runner-up four times.

Snead was another legend who made his mark at Augusta during those years. He won the Masters three times from 1949 to 1954. If anyone could rival Hogan for consistency, it was Snead. From 1939 to 1957, he played in the Masters 16 times. Snead finished in the top eight 13 times. In addition to his three wins, he had four other top-three finishes during those years.

Demaret found great success at the Masters, too. He won the event in 1940, 1947, and 1950. That made him the first three-time Masters champion. Demaret needed some good fortune to win in 1950. Jim Ferrier had the lead

## Getting into Augusta

Most players consider it an honor just to be able to play at the Masters. It is not easy getting in. Most players have to reach a certain qualification. Over the years, the list of qualifications has changed or been modified several times. Technically, players must receive an invitation to play. As of 2012, however, there were 19 ways to earn an automatic invitation. Among the qualifications:

★ Past Masters champions are always eligible for play

★ The top 16 players from the previous year are eligible

★ Winners of the US Open, British Open, and PGA Championship are eligible for five years

★ The top 50 players on the Official World Golf Ranking are eligible

Ben Hogan hits out of a sand trap on the second hole of the Masters in 1954. He won the tournament in 1951 and 1953.

going into the final day. But Ferrier stumbled during the final nine holes. Demaret took advantage to win by two strokes.

From 1946 to 1959, seven different future Hall of Famers won the Masters. Hogan, Snead, and Demaret were among them. The others were Cary Middlecoff (1955), Burke Jr. (1956), Doug Ford (1957), and Palmer (1958).

After shooting a solid 72 in the first round in 1955, Middlecoff fired off a 65 in round two. That included just 31 strokes on the front nine, a stretch that included four consecutive birdies. Middlecoff went into the

## Dinner Time

A new tradition at the Masters began in 1952. Ben Hogan wrote a letter to Clifford Roberts and suggested that all the past champions gather for a dinner during the week of the tournament. The tradition was born. Today past champions and club members attend the dinner two nights before the start of the tournament. They all wear their green jackets. The previous year's champion selects the menu. That has led to some interesting dishes over the years. Haggis, elk, and bobotie, which is a South African dish, are among the most memorable foods served at the Champions Dinner.

final round with a four-shot lead over Hogan. That lead only grew when Hogan missed several key putts early on. With the pressure off, Middlecoff coasted to the win. He finished the four-day event at 9-under par 279. The seven-stroke margin of victory was the largest in the first 28 Masters.

Middlecoff nearly won again in 1959. Wall Jr. delivered one of the greatest finishes in golf history, though. He birdied five of the final six holes to defeat Middlecoff by a single stroke. Wall Jr. passed 12 players on the leader board during his final flurry.

## The Masters Continues to Grow

In addition to showcasing great players, the Masters hit some milestones during those years. The first leader boards were built in 1947.

## Amen Corner

The most famous stretch at Augusta National is holes 11, 12, and 13. Many Masters have been won or lost on that difficult stretch of play. All three holes feature potentially dangerous water hazards or bunkers and have ruined many scorecards. Playing well on those holes, however, can be a major boost for a player. In 1958, *Sports Illustrated* writer Herbert Warren Wind nicknamed that stretch "Amen Corner." The name stuck and has contributed to making that part of the course so revered today.

Ike's Pond and two other ponds were added to the grounds. The par-3 course was built in 1958. One of the tournament's great traditions began in 1949. That was the first year that a green jacket was awarded to the winner. Snead was the first player to earn one.

Television also came to Augusta during that era. In 1956, CBS broadcast the Masters for the first time. Only 2.5 hours were shown. The coverage was not nearly as complete as it is today. But golf fans loved it. Approximately 10 million people watched around the country. Through 2012, CBS had broadcast the Masters every year since 1956.

As the 1950s came to a close, the Masters had become wildly popular. The crowds were huge and the great moments were greater than ever. As great as those years were, however, the future looked even brighter.

Some of golf's greats had seen their best days. Demaret, Hogan, and Snead had all dominated the sport for years. But they did not routinely contend at the Masters anymore. They passed the torch to a younger set of stars, led by Palmer.

Palmer followed up his 1958 win with a third-place finish in 1959. He was just getting started, though. The 1960s would see a new level of excellence for Palmer, the sport of golf, and the Masters.

# Palmer, Nicklaus Take Over

Professional golf has witnessed some good rivalries over the years. Hogan v. Snead. Woods v. Mickelson. Jones v. Hagen.

Perhaps none could ever match the battles between Jack Nicklaus and Arnold Palmer, however. During the 1960s and 1970s, Nicklaus and Palmer were the kings of golf—and the best of the best at the Masters.

Palmer actually won his first Masters in 1958. But he added three more wins from 1960 to 1964. He played in his first Masters in 1955,

**Arnold Palmer hits out of a sand trap on the first hole at Augusta National at the 1959 Masters.**

## Quite a Player

Had it not been for Jack Nicklaus and Arnold Palmer, Gary Player might have been considered the greatest golfer of the 1960s and 1970s. From 1959 to 1978, Player won nine major titles. That included three wins at the Masters, in 1961, 1974, and 1978. In fact, from 1959 to 1979, Player had 14 top-10 finishes at the Masters—just two fewer than Nicklaus. Prior to 1980, the South African was the only international player to win the Masters.

finishing in a tie for tenth. From 1957 to 1967, Palmer had 11 consecutive top-10 finishes. Included were his four wins.

"I've always made a total effort, even when the odds seemed entirely against me," Palmer said in 1960. "I never quit trying; I never felt that I didn't have a chance to win."

Nicklaus must have felt the same way as he piled up 22 top-10 finishes at Augusta. Through 2012, Nicklaus was the only six-time winner of the Masters. Palmer and Tiger Woods were the only other players with at least four Masters wins.

In 1964, Palmer won his fourth Masters, while Nicklaus finished second. The next year, Nicklaus won, while Palmer was second. Both were in the top four in 1966, when Nicklaus won. It became common to see

Jack Nicklaus helped the Masters and golf in general grow during the 1960s, when he won seven majors including the 1963, 1965, and 1966 Masters.

one slip the green jacket onto the back of the other. Palmer and Nicklaus combined to win the Masters five years in a row from 1962 to 1966.

Palmer was golf's first everyman star. Fans adored him for his working-class background and likeable personality. That is to say nothing of his dominant golf game. Many credit Palmer for sparking golf's boost in popularity during the 1960s. He made golf feel like a sport everybody

## Ike at Augusta

Dwight D. Eisenhower, president of the United States from 1953 to 1961, had a deep connection to Augusta National. Eisenhower, nicknamed "Ike," became a member of the club in 1948. He was a member for the rest of his life. Although he passed away in 1969, his legacy lives on. Ike's Pond, now located on the club's par-3 course, was named after him. So was Eisenhower Cabin, a house built near the 10th tee for Eisenhower and his wife in 1953. Another landmark in his honor is the Eisenhower Tree on the 17th fairway. The former president hit that tree multiple times with bad shots when he played the course. In fact, he actually asked that the tree be removed, but his request was denied.

Eisenhower never attended the Masters as president. Instead, he arrived the Monday after the tournament to play a round with the new champion and other club members.

could play, not just society's elite. That was reflected in the fans in the gallery who followed him around at tournaments. They became known as Arnie's Army.

Palmer was golf's biggest star when Nicklaus debuted as a professional. Nicklaus, who was 10 years younger than Palmer, quickly proved to be a worthy rival. The two shared the spotlight for several years before the younger Nicklaus took Palmer's spot as the unquestioned best player in the game. Like Palmer, he became wildly popular.

They finished their careers as two of the most successful golfers ever. Both were major reasons why golf grew so much in popularity during the 1960s and 1970s. And when their prime years overlapped, the two stars thrived on beating each other.

"My first concern is to win, of course," Nicklaus said before the 1965 Masters, "but I also try awfully hard to beat Arnold. If he finishes fiftieth in a tournament, then I darn sure want to finish at least forty-ninth."

Palmer and Nicklaus never did have a great head-to-head battle at the Masters. Yet it was the potential for greatness by at least one of them that made them so popular. Often one of them delivered that greatness, and millions got the chance to watch.

The emergence of Palmer and Nicklaus happened as golf was becoming a popular sport on television. Fans around the United States could finally watch the big tournaments from the comfort of their homes. Palmer and Nicklaus were the first big stars during those years.

On the course, few could match their success. Nicklaus won 73 PGA Tour events and 18 major championships. Palmer won 62 PGA Tour events and seven majors. For years, they were fierce competitors, but they also had great respect for one another.

Nicklaus said of Palmer: "Arnold treated me great. He couldn't have been nicer. He's always been that way with me."

By 2012, it had been decades since either man had challenged for the Masters title. However, they were still as popular as ever with the fans.

They were especially popular with the fans at Augusta National. Palmer, after all, played in the Masters 50 straight years from 1955 to 2004. Nicklaus played in the Masters 45 times from 1959 to 2005.

"Augusta and this golf tournament has been about [as much] a part of my life as anything other than my family," Palmer said after playing his final Masters in 2004.

In 2010, Nicklaus said, "I have had such a long-standing appreciation and love affair with Augusta National and the Masters Tournament."

## New Traditions

Throughout the 1960s and 1970s, there were plenty of landmark moments at the Masters. The first par-3 contest took place in 1960. It is now an annual tradition played the day before the first round on a nearby par-3 course. Honorary starters were first used in 1963. That tradition began out of a desire to celebrate past Masters greats. The starters hit a ceremonial first drive at the beginning of each tournament. In 1965, Butler Cabin was used for the green jacket presentation on CBS television for the first time. That year, Palmer gave the jacket to Nicklaus. A year later, in 1966, the Masters was shown on television in color for the first time. Sudden death playoffs were introduced in 1976.

That era also produced many memorable performances. From 1966 to 1970, the tournament was decided by just one stroke (twice in a playoff)

Defending Masters champion Arnold Palmer, *right*, places the traditional green jacket on 1965 Masters champion Jack Nicklaus, who shot a record 17-under par.

five years in a row. Raymond Floyd had one of the most dominating performances in tournament history in 1976. He finished at 17-under par and won by eight strokes. That score tied Nicklaus's record from 1965. Through 2012, that was still the third-largest margin of victory in Masters history. Floyd was also just the fourth wire-to-wire winner—something nobody has done since.

Hall of Famers Tommy Aaron, Billy Casper, Gary Player, and Tom Watson were among the Masters champs during the 1960s and 1970s.

PALMER, NICKLAUS TAKE OVER

Jack Nicklaus and his caddie celebrate after Nicklaus sank a birdie on the 15th hole at the 1966 Masters. Nicklaus won his third Masters that year.

Nothing in those 20 years, however, could match the dominance of Nicklaus and Palmer. They provided many of the greatest moments in tournament history.

In 1958, Palmer sank an eagle on hole 13 to set up his first Masters victory. His back-to-back birdies on the final two holes in 1960 sealed another win. Palmer's 1962 win might have been his most dramatic. He went into the final round with the lead, only to struggle early and fall behind. A late run helped him draw even with Player and Dow Finsterwald on the final hole. Then a slow start in the next day's three-way playoff left Palmer down three strokes after nine holes.

That is when Palmer showed his greatness. Within five holes, Palmer went from a three-stroke deficit to a four-stroke lead. His 68 round easily beat Player's 71 and Finsterwald's 77 to take the title.

Palmer's most dominating Masters performance was in 1964. He entered the final round with a four-shot lead. He ended six strokes ahead of second-place Dave Marr at 12-under par.

By then, however, Palmer was getting older. Nicklaus, meanwhile, was just getting started. The 23-year-old had a lukewarm start at the 1963 Masters, shooting 74. Only three times in tournament history had the winner shot over par on the first day. But after a scorching 66 on day two, Nicklaus was on his way to becoming the youngest Masters champion. Years later, in 1986, he became the oldest Masters champion at age 46.

In between Nicklaus won four more Masters titles. He wowed the field with a stunning 17-under par to win in 1965. Then he became the first back-to-back champion by winning a playoff in1966. His dramatic 40-foot birdie putt on the 16th hole during the final round in 1975 helped him to a one-shot victory—his fifth win at Augusta.

They were superstars and they were rivals. Palmer and Nicklaus will forever be remembered as two of the greatest champions in Masters history.

# International Flavor

The 1961 Masters was significant for a couple of reasons. For one, it was a rare look at Arnold Palmer losing a tournament. He was going for his second straight Masters win. And he had a one-shot lead heading into the final hole. However, the legend made a double bogey on 18 to lose. It was also significant because champion Gary Player was from South Africa. He was the first foreign-born golfer to win the Masters. Player would go on to win the Masters two more times, in 1974 and 1978.

Gary Player of South Africa reacts after making a birdie on the sixth hole at the 1961 Masters. He became the first international Masters champion that year.

During the first 43 Masters tournaments, from 1934 to 1979, Player was the only foreign-born golfer to win. The tournament went to US players 40 times in those 43 tournaments.

"It was a very important thing," Player said of being the first international winner at the Masters, "because it gave encouragement for many to follow suit. There's an international player who can do it. It was really not the desire then to play around the world."

## Going Global

From 1980 to 2000, international players won the Masters 12 times. Meanwhile, US players won it just nine times during that span. The winners in those two decades came from seven countries, including the United States. Some of the great international players in golf history won a green jacket in those years. Nick Faldo of England won it three times.

Seve Ballesteros and Jose Maria Olazabal of Spain, and Bernhard Langer of Germany each won it twice.

Ballesteros was the first to break through after Player. In 1980, the Spaniard became the first European to win at the Masters. At that time, he also became the youngest champion in tournament history. The 23-year-old Ballesteros was dominant in finishing at 13-under par. He won by four strokes for his first green jacket.

Three years after his first title, Ballesteros became the tenth player to win at least two Masters. Ballesteros earned a reputation for being one of the top players in the world. During the 1980s, he won four major tournaments and had 15 top-10 finishes. Seven of those were at the

## US Winners

While international players dominated the 1980s and 1990s, US players had fun at the Masters, too. Ben Crenshaw won the event twice in those years, in 1984 and 1995. Tom Watson won his second green jacket in 1981 (he also won in 1977) and Jack Nicklaus won his sixth, in 1986. Tiger Woods won his first jacket in 1997. Fred Couples, Mark O'Meara, Craig Stadler, and Augusta native Larry Mize also won the Masters in those years.

Masters. "On a golf course Seve's got everything. I mean everything: touch, power, know-how, courage, and charisma," fellow Hall of Famer Lee Trevino said.

Langer was the only German champ in tournament history through 2012. He won in 1985 and 1993 for the only major wins of his Hall of Fame career. Langer had never won a tournament on US soil before his win in 1985. In both of his Masters wins, Langer used a furious rally on the back nine on Sunday to claim victory.

Olazabal brought the title back to Spain in 1994 and again in 1999. He drained a stellar 30-foot eagle putt on the 15th hole in the final round in 1994. That gave him a two-shot lead over Tom Lehman with three holes to play. The eagle was big because Lehman would close the gap to one going to 18. Olazabal needed a good chip shot to set up a par putt that sealed the win. In 1999, Olazabal bogeyed three straight holes early in the final round. But he recovered to go 4-under par during the final 13 holes, winning by two shots.

## An Elite Englishman

Faldo topped them all by winning three green jackets from 1989 to 1996. The Englishman did not just win, however. He won in dramatic fashion every time. In each of his Masters wins, Faldo went into the final round trailing by several strokes.

In 1989, Faldo faced a five-shot deficit going into the final round. The three players ahead of Faldo going into Sunday all played well. Ben Crenshaw was 1-under par in the final round. Scott Hoch was 3-under and Greg Norman was 5-under. Faldo, however, put together a remarkable 7-under 65 in the final round.

Hoch and Crenshaw were still on the course when Faldo finished. Both went into the final hole tied with Faldo at 5-under. But Crenshaw bogeyed to fall out of contention. Hoch came just inches shy of sinking a birdie putt that would have won.

Hoch made par to force a playoff with Faldo. And Hoch had a chance to win on the first extra hole. But he missed a two-foot putt. When Faldo birdied on the next hole, the green jacket was his.

Faldo joined Jack Nicklaus in 1990 as the only players at that time to win back-to-back Masters championships. He also became the first player to win two sudden-death playoffs for the green jacket. Faldo trailed Raymond Floyd by three shots going into the final round. In fact, he trailed by four with six holes to play. But Faldo birdied holes 13, 15, and 16 to pull within one shot. Then Floyd bogeyed 17, dropping into a tie with Faldo. The tie held, forcing a playoff. And like in 1989, Faldo needed just two playoff holes to win.

Faldo's win in 1996 was one of the most remarkable results in Masters history. Australian Greg Norman had dominated the first three rounds.

He took a commanding six-stroke lead into the final round. That final round has gone down in Masters lore.

Throughout the front nine, Faldo chipped away at Norman's lead. Norman bogeyed three holes in the front nine. After three straight bogeys to open the back nine, the tournament was tied. Norman's bad luck only continued. He hit a shot on 12 that fell short of the green and bounced into the water, resulting in a double bogey. Faldo never let up the pressure, and Norman continued to fold. When the round was over, Faldo had turned a six-stroke deficit into a five-shot victory. Faldo carded a 5-under 67 for the day, while Norman finished with a 6-over 78.

## Heartache for Norman

Australian Greg Norman won two majors in his career, but he became most known for his stunning losses at the Masters. His epic collapse on the back nine at the 1996 Masters was just one of many.

In 1986, Norman took a one-shot lead into the final round. However, he struggled early and lost to Jack Nicklaus by one stroke. In 1987, Norman missed a birdie putt on the 18th green that would have won. That sent him into a three-way playoff. On the second playoff hole, Larry Mize drained a stunning 140-foot chip shot that left Norman empty-handed again.

In the 1989 final round, Norman made six birdies in nine holes, from 9 to 17. Then he mishit his second shot on 18. That was followed by a poor chip shot and a missed 12-foot putt for par. His bogey on 18 caused him to miss a playoff by one shot.

Following his final putt—a birdie, of course—Faldo hugged Norman. The 1996 Masters is still known as much for Norman's collapse as it is for Faldo's rally. Both players seemed to realize that in the moment. "Amazing. I don't know how it happened," Faldo said afterward. "He had played so great. It was the strangest turn of events I've ever seen. I genuinely feel for the guy. I feel so sad for him."

The dramatic finish aside, the 1996 Masters was a classic example of how far international players had come. England's Faldo defeated Australia's Norman, while Frank Nobilo of New Zealand was fourth.

## Nicklaus Charges to Victory

While foreign players made their mark during those years, an old favorite shined, too. Jack Nicklaus came into the 1986 Masters with five green jackets. At 46 years old, nobody thought he could win another.

He played well in the first three rounds. Still, he was four shots back and in a tie for ninth entering the final round. But Nicklaus carded a 7-under 65 in the final round. That included a three-hole stretch of eagle-birdie-birdie late in his round. With his son, Jackie, caddying for him, Nicklaus secured his sixth green jacket. It was his eighteenth and final major win. Nicklaus became the oldest winner in Masters history. "I think what it did was put an exclamation point on my career," Nicklaus said.

## Looking Forward

From 1980 to 2000, international players made a major impact on Augusta. Sandy Lyle was the first Scottish player to win the event in 1988. Ian Woosnam of Wales won in 1991. In 2000, Vijay Singh, from the island of Fiji, claimed the green jacket.

The Masters was no longer just an American event. It had international flavor all over its annual leader board. Players from Ireland, Italy, Japan, South Africa, Zimbabwe, and elsewhere in the world routinely finished among the top 10. The trend has continued ever since. The boom of international stars in the 1980s and 1990s changed the face of golf, and the Masters, forever.

# The Masters Today

Every era in Masters history has had star players. Since 1997, two players have controlled Augusta: Tiger Woods and Phil Mickelson.

Woods won his first Masters in 1997. Then, from 2001 to 2010, Woods and Mickelson combined to win six of the 10 green jackets. For several years, Woods was the most dominant player in golf. He made a habit out of contending at major tournaments, especially the Masters. In 2001 and 2002, Woods won the Masters in back-to-back years. He joined Jack Nicklaus and Nick Faldo as the only players to pull off that feat.

Phil Mickelson chips on the first fairway during first-round play at the 2004 Masters. He won his first major that year at Augusta.

# Lefty Gets Going

As great as Woods has been at Augusta National, Mickelson has been almost as good. He got off to a slow start, though. Mickelson in 2004 had a reputation for being one of the game's great players. But he had never won a major tournament. He was labeled as "the greatest player to never win a major."

At the 2004 Masters, Mickelson changed that label. And he did it with one of the greatest putts in tournament history. Mickelson was tied with Ernie Els when he stepped onto the 18th green. He stared at an 18-foot birdie putt that could win the tournament. The left-handed Mickelson tapped the ball. Then he watched it roll toward the cup. It finally dropped in and "Lefty" had his first major.

"It was an amazing, amazing day, the fulfillment of all my dreams," Mickelson said.

Winning the Masters was a turning point in Mickelson's career. He won another major, the PGA Championship, in 2005. Then, he won the Masters again in 2006 and 2010. He became one of just eight players to win at least three Masters. In 2012, Mickelson tied for third—his fourteenth top-10 finish since 1995.

"I'm in love with this place; it brings out the best in me," Mickelson said after his win in 2010.

## Another Win for Woods

Woods's win in 2005 featured one of the most dramatic shots in Masters history. He faced a chip shot from off the green on the par-3 16th hole. It was such a difficult shot that even Woods figured his best hope was to get it close and putt for par.

Woods's club struck the ball and it landed several feet above the hole. Then it took a sharp turn to the right. It slowly rolled toward the cup, paused on the lip, and then dropped in for a birdie.

The tournament was not over yet. Woods lost his two-stroke lead with back-to-back bogeys on 17 and 18. He finally claimed the title after beating Chris DiMarco on the first playoff hole.

That win entered Woods into a select group. Woods (four), Arnold Palmer (four), and Nicklaus (six) are the only players to win the tournament at least four times. Through 2012, Woods had 12 top-10 finishes in the 16 Masters he had played as a professional.

## Expect the Unexpected

The Masters has a way of bringing out the best in a lot of players. The great ones—such as Nicklaus, Palmer, Woods, Mickelson, and Player— have made Augusta National an annual grand stage.

Over the years, however, the Masters has seen a lot of lesser-known players come though. Bubba Watson certainly fit on that list. Unlike most professionals, Watson did not take golf lessons and did not have a swing coach. He did things his way. In 2012, that led to four straight birdies on the back nine in the final round. Watson wound up in a tie with Louis Oosthuizen.

On the second playoff hole, Watson sailed his tee shot into a forest of trees. He appeared doomed. Then he came up with the shot of the tournament. Watson hit an unusual hook out of the trees. It traveled 155 yards and landed 15 feet from the hole. Watson then made his fourth shot to secure the victory.

Watson was the latest in a long line of unpredictable winners. Mickelson and Woods won five of the six Masters from 2001 to 2006. Six different players won the six tournaments after that. Zach Johnson (2007),

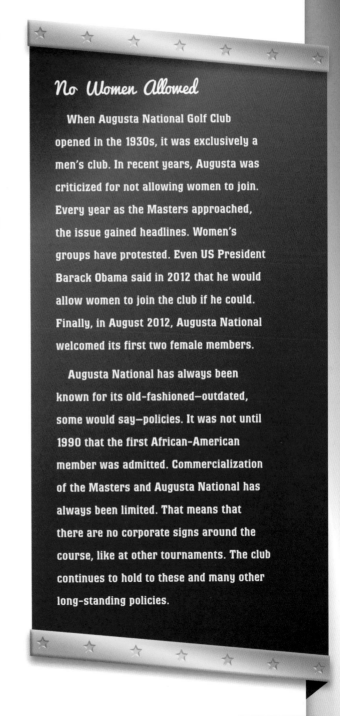

## No Women Allowed

When Augusta National Golf Club opened in the 1930s, it was exclusively a men's club. In recent years, Augusta was criticized for not allowing women to join. Every year as the Masters approached, the issue gained headlines. Women's groups have protested. Even US President Barack Obama said in 2012 that he would allow women to join the club if he could. Finally, in August 2012, Augusta National welcomed its first two female members.

Augusta National has always been known for its old-fashioned—outdated, some would say—policies. It was not until 1990 that the first African-American member was admitted. Commercialization of the Masters and Augusta National has always been limited. That means that there are no corporate signs around the course, like at other tournaments. The club continues to hold to these and many other long-standing policies.

Trevor Immelman (2008), Charl Schwartzel (2011), and Watson (2012) each won his first major at the Masters. Angel Cabrera won his second major title in 2009 after a three-way playoff.

Augusta National has come a long way since the Fruitland Nurseries occupied the land in the early 1930s. The course is now one of the most famous in the world. The Masters is one of the most sacred tournaments in golf. Winning this tournament often defines a player and gives him a memory he'll never forget.

"As an athlete and golfer, this is the mecca," Watson said after his playoff win in 2012. "This is what we strive for, to put on the green jacket. . . . This is an honor, a special privilege to put the green jacket on."

Bubba Watson watches a putt during the third round of the 2012 Masters. He won fans over with his unorthodox style and surprising Masters win.

# TIMELINE

Augusta National Golf Club officially opens. Technically play began in 1932.
**1933**

The Masters is held for the first time, with Horton Smith winning the tournament.
**1934**

The tournament, formerly called Augusta National Invitation Tournament, is officially renamed "The Masters."
**1939**

The Masters is cancelled because of World War II. It remains cancelled through 1945.
**1943**

The green jacket is awarded to the winner for the first time. Sam Snead wins the first jacket.
**1949**

Arnold Palmer wins the Masters for the fourth time—the first player to accomplish that feat.
**1964**

Jack Nicklaus wins his second straight Masters, becoming the first to win it two years in a row.
**1966**

Seve Ballesteros is the first European to win the Masters. From 1980 to 1999, European players won the event 11 times.
**1980**

Nicklaus wins his record sixth Masters. In doing so, the 46-year-old becomes the oldest Masters champion.
**1986**

Greg Norman loses a six-shot lead in the final round. Nick Faldo takes advantage to earn his third Masters title.
**1996**

**Jimmy Demaret** becomes the first three-time champion in Masters history.

**1950**

**Sam Snead** wins his third Masters. It is the fourth year in a row that either Snead or Ben Hogan, two of golf's greats, won the event.

**1954**

The Masters is televised for the first time. CBS has televised the tournament every year since then through 2012.

**1956**

The par-3 contest, which has become an annual tradition, is held for the first time.

**1960**

**Gary Player**, from South Africa, is the first international winner.

**1961**

**Tiger Woods**, 21, becomes the youngest Masters champ. He also sets a new scoring record and has the widest margin of victory in tournament history.

**1997**

Woods wins for the second year in a row. He joins Nicklaus and Faldo as the only players to win in back-to-back years.

**2002**

**Phil Mickelson** wins his first Masters. He would win again in 2006 and 2010.

**2004**

Woods wins his fourth Masters, joining Palmer and Nicklaus as the only players to win it that many times.

**2005**

**Bubba Watson** wins the Masters by winning the ninth sudden-death playoff in tournament history.

**2012**

## The Trophy

Each year, the Masters champion receives a green jacket, a gold medal, and a trophy. The main trophy is a small model of the clubhouse. It is permanently displayed at Augusta National.

## The Legends

**Phil Mickelson (United States):** Three wins, beginning in 2004.

**Jack Nicklaus (United States):** Six wins from 1963 to 1986.

**Arnold Palmer (United States):** Four wins from 1958 to 1964.

**Sam Snead (United States):** Three wins from 1949 to 1954.

**Tiger Woods (United States):** Four wins, beginning in 1997.

## The Venue

Augusta National Golf Club was opened in 1932. It features several famous ponds and bridges. It is also well-known for the different plants around the course. Each hole is named for a plant featured on that hole. The most famous stretch of holes is 11, 12, and 13—the "Amen Corner."

# GLOSSARY

**amateur**
A player who does not benefit financially from competition.

**birdie**
Finishing a hole at 1-under par.

**bogey**
Finishing a hole at 1-over par.

**bunkers**
Sand traps located throughout a golf course.

**contention**
When a golfer is close enough to the leader to have a chance to win.

**eagle**
Finishing at hole at 2-under par.

**gallery**
The spectators at a golf tournament.

**lore**
Knowledge or traditions of a subject.

**majors**
Four tournaments that are regarded as the elite tournaments on golf's schedule every year.

**par**
The number of strokes that a golfer should need to finish a hole or a round of golf.

**prodigy**
A person, usually young, who shows remarkable talent.

**reputation**
The way in which a person is viewed by others.

**revered**
To be held in high regard by others.

## FOR MORE INFORMATION

## Selected Bibliography

Barrett, Ted with Chris Hawkes. *The Complete Encyclopedia of Golf*. New York: Sterling Publishing Co., 2010.

Uschan, Michael V. *History of Sports: Golf*. San Diego, CA: Lucent Books, 2001.

## Further Readings

Barrett, David. *Making the Masters: Bobby Jones and the Birth of America's Greatest Golf Tournament*. New York: Skyhorse Publishing, 2012.

Christian, Frank. *Augusta National & The Masters: A Photographer's Scrapbook*. Charleston, S.C.: BookSurge Publishing, 2009.

Green Sr., Ron. *The Masters: 101 Reasons to Love Golf's Greatest Tournament*. New York: Stewart, Tabori & Chang, 2008.

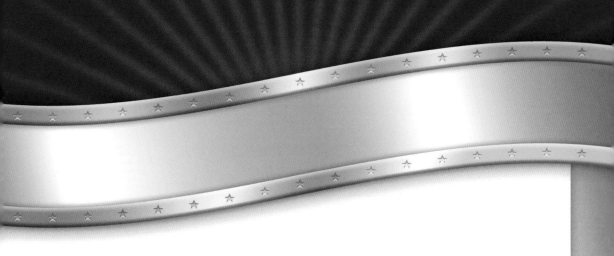

## Web Links

To learn more about the Masters, visit ABDO Publishing Company online at **www.abdopublishing.com**. Web sites about the Masters are featured on our Book Links page. These links are routinely monitored and updated to provide the most current information available.

## Places to Visit

**Augusta National Golf Club**
2604 Washington Road, Augusta, GA 30904
(706) 667-6000
**www.masters.com**
Augusta National Golf Club is one of the world's most famous golf courses and has been home to the Masters since its beginning in 1934. As a private club, it is closed to visitors outside of the Masters.

**World Golf Hall of Fame**
One World Golf Place, St. Augustine, FL 32092
(904) 940-4123
**www.worldgolfhalloffame.org**
This hall of fame and museum features exhibits that chronicle the history of golf as well as hands-on activities for visitors to learn more about the sport. Tickets to the hall of fame also include access to an IMAX film and an 18-hole putting course.

# INDEX

## About the Author

Brian Howell is a freelance writer based in Denver, Colorado. He has been a sports journalist for nearly 20 years, writing about high school, college, and professional athletics. In addition, he has written books about sports and history. A native of Colorado, he lives with his wife and four children.